The Violence of the Morning

The Violence of the Morning

Poems by Cal Bedient

The University of Georgia Press

Athens and London

Published by the University of Georgia Press

Athens, Georgia 30602

© 2002 by Cal Bedient

Set in 9.5 on 14 Bodoni by Bookcomp, Inc.

Printed and bound by McNaughton and Gunn, Inc.

The paper in this book meets the guidelines for
permanence and durability of the Committee on
Production Guidelines for Book Longevity of the
Council on Library Resources.

Printed in the United States of America

06 05 04 03 02 P 5 4 3 2 1

Library of Congress Cataloging-in-Publication Data

Bedient, Calvin.

    The violence of the morning : poems / by Cal Bedient.

        p. cm.

    ISBN 0-8203-2390-X (alk. paper)

    1. Title.

    PS3552.E314 V56 2002

    811'.54—dc21   2001008253

British Library Cataloging-in-Publication Data available

Contents

4.

1.

Minotaur Provides for This Paragraph

The ground [. . .] very much eating.
My death is the breathing in the flower.
Pretty thing, chopped up around its center. Edible.
      Somewhere above.

I close my eyes and walk out into the city on all fours,
And on to the meadow. (Why, it blushes to see me!)
And give myself over to

          [replaced by:]

It's useless. I get a dirty feeling right here.
I think these nerve endings are not nice.

My friends!
          [*in the margins:* sacrificed]

Stand up, pulse, I say, even if one leg is a field
And another a condor—I talk to myself this way
To keep

      off the smells of jagged, discursive life.

Look behind the first edition: air
         petting the blackberries.
They have nothing on us now.

         The stories I'd tell my children:
The library opens at 10. The regulations
I'd pass on to them.
  [crossed out]

My friends!
I shall get to the heart of it all presently.
I've been put where
I've been given the plan of

Plus the outside isn't in relationship, really.
        [*illegible: crossed out*]

We give next these scattered notes:

Herodotus was wrong about an Egyptian
        reputed to have the loudest voice in the world.
I myself have filled these 14 miles of corridors with the sounds of troops
             shouting as they kill,
And my mother was human, I should not be overlooked.

Dilating in darkness to be born again [*crossed out*]

Blind creature
        [*start again:*]

O love [*start again:*]

Her heare was yellow as the gold, she was a jolly Dame.
And stoutly served mee, and I did love her for the same.

Verse is my passion. It gets me out of heare.
I sway my rump and get off my thoughts [. . .]

        For I was thither come, ta dum.
I saw how from the slivered flowres red drops of blood did fall,
And how that shuddring horribly the branches—

I was addicted to rage, the doctors said.
It gave me a funny look. My father called me names.
Penis envy, probably.

[start again:]

Ah, mee. I cannot stay focused in this gloom.
I SAW THE MILLIONS OF DATA CROWDED ON THE HEAD OF A PIN.
This was a dream. I WAS SHOT INTO SPACE. This was a dream.
Bollocks-brained, the doctors said.
Asses, I blew them apart with one scream.

How many feet of sod on my roof?
Sometimes I think I heare rain.
I patch together from the tarnished silver sounds
A slithery suit of glitter-scales.
Oh, ladies, run your hands along my spine.
Yes, yes, pet Mino, only a wild destruction shines.

[on the other side:] Death is in a sense an imposture
[crossed out]

And when the book is finished, after which I

Tons of flesh and its stupidity *[stop?]*

The collapse of time within me, filthy—

[. . .] bite the outstretched hand.

Was It Stella, or Was It Stella?

You're safe, you think—as a train,
three-quarters across a toothpick trestle,
is already a pinker worm.

The mind takes off its shoes.
Between the sheets is maybe squeezed
and pleased. And on the bedside table,

thirty-three verselets of desolation.
What a day it was. You've been to history—
Murillo's hag

raising the curtain of the young girl's skirt
to hawk her skinny tush
like a still-wet painting:

beauty, you thought,
had ampler proportions.
Was the day Stella, as in your aunt,

intimate as "insides,"
or as in Frank's
brittle geometries—the squared-off planks

still tingling from the logging
of the sacred grove?
Was there even a moment

when beauty massaged the roast be
of every color in the garden?
(A thing like that, doesn't cover herself.)

Listen, I know about not shifting

suddenly, but stand in this frame
and see what you've missed
because you weren't a work of art—

so little, a zoo of faces and spectacles;
and when the guard turns out the lights,
you'll strain to hear his shoes

squeak like an after-hours sex doll
in the one-inch Christmas cotton.
A still thing has no pleasure, so laugh

as you leave the house tomorrow,
a fork going somewhere lovely
in a bamboo picnic basket,

close by a jar of diced beets
in vinaigrette and tarragon.
But now it's night, the mouth-hole

closes over the verb. For the first time today,
you include yourself, like a liquid
capsule that sleep will swallow. Still,

you're up late again, I see,
and with a certain authority.
I praise you. I praise you.

Out of the Woods Come Armies and Sexual Feeling

Why does one want to paint the ears canna-lilied like that?
Aren't they already there, canna-lilied like that?
No, flame-shaped. No, supposing.
Supposing there is danger.

The doe hides in the woods while Corot,
smock-whited frog prince, daubs with a tongue just as long
as any song, oh lush as any sponge is his sop up.
His is to add down the colored mud the way Arcadian.

What the afternoon does he does it does what he does
like coming into a station. Up through a thousand images,
all traces, he climbs like a bee on a lemon,
till a transparent yellow god dreams the wriggling tree trunks,

sallow glassy gold light on the bark—a dream
more real than the dreamer, where trees raise
burly leaf-backs against the water-rush of blue.

But what is not inside, actually, as to that,
ever? Even the leaves, part dew part ash, luff and languish,
as time is extra and union. Found lately. Found now
as a fine lady who sits naked before him,

hips wide as six babies bundled together. She looks
at him as at a slightly annoying whine in the air.
It is his pipe, perhaps, smelling of burning summer
and cottages, and by and by. A tall girl leans back on a tree

as if it had grown there to support her—in her hands
a book blond as a chip chopped with one blow from an oak.

She's inside the inside, and so outside it, dreamily,
where one cannot see the other dream, like a soldier

hoping to get a letter. Inside the painter's pants,
a branchy poke, remote as a blue militia
on the next hill. Ignore it: what is not as equitable as individual
is not in the sweetness of the dream. How to tilt the maid's

big-lashed moon head over her lady, as if to hear
the earth below? Ooh la la the sweet kernel hum
somewhere down in musk mallow time.
——The khaki light unstraps its belt,

the Frenchwomen stretch mais oui to mine if mine
and unreceived. Misarranged and suited. Off canvas.
Muscles back to the change of that: the next in.
Chattering, the little group exits the holiday

greenery. Now she comes forward,
the small-ankled deer. Hotter than any bush. Her tail,
like a rifle, jerks. Jerks again. Her ears like leaves apt to fall.
No, not like. Not extra. No one's dream.

Jove's Thunder But a Murmur in the Leaves

——odor of hot stone, like a sibyl
       ironing, is it not so, her duns and indigos
          . . .
       odor of love   sea ammonia

——a licknut leaf diving out after boyish pleasures,
     ·   as Apollo hung out
   whole days with Hyacinthus—jack-juice
outlaws:

    . one of them the green sometimes seen in flames;
         the other, the green of lime sherbet—

and then there was an accident

——To know is reckless emphasis, a white tablecloth
               (oh killed)
     under trees, the caterpillar gods
       vast in their gauzy hammocks

——Wind's wristsends so lightly dove the candidacy
    of wingless vines. Hunger in the tendril:
     front
    runner of a great many mouths.

"Dionysus becomes visible in emerald beauty."

——we have looked for ourselves in the sull-, in the puzz-,

who sow in a floating field,
nor stalkstink nor preyweld.

"Oh friends, what have we done?"

"Dolphins crowned with vine branches of foam"

Go to the Middle of Anything, It Is a River

1

. . . appointed so as not to be too wide . . .

I curl the pencil's hair in the sharpener—blow on its blonde.
    Like a merry—a constant—girl, the rabbit electrical

light smells my spine. Sunshine is many come.
    Who marries the green side of the air? Bee is appointed,

so as not to let it be—too wide. You program off—
    you stumpy dark—have you missed your appointed?

Is your life like a running horse—with a foot
    in each instant?

I've tied it so often—I'll tie it no more—

2

. . . I say to the hum, bist du mein? . . .

Was irritated by now. Said "go" to the paint brush
    dragging the invisible. Said "no" to the girls

alligatoring in the dust. All is a come to fears—
    unappointed ahead—unappointed behind.

"*Bist du,*" asked Berli—in the Windemere—retention camp—
    "*bist du mein?* You must never leave your children,

always you must stay with them." The smallest boy
  crawled up the curtain and hissed.

I think I love you, mother, like a station—where one passenger—waits—

3

  . . . Chardin's man blows worlds out the window, o . . .

I say to the sky circle, *bist du mein?* I thank I love the scalp-up
  of the air. Mother clouds. Flock breasts of light.

Will you know me, mother? Do not trust this photo,
  I cannot look portrait from a train.

I am breath—film of earth—boy aired—boy expendable.
  Trailing his stick leg up the curtain, o.

Spitting Jew! "No," said the sparrow, "I won't make a stew."
  So he clapped his wings, and away he flew.

He flew—and he flew—and he flew.

4

  . . . pain brush dragging the visible for its dead . . .

I once for the wind cried in the grater pines—twice
  for the tiger lily spattered my blood. Said "Oh!"

to the hermaphrodite sailor—scratching his stubble—
  if this be *he.* Lost his baby overboard? Couldn't be!

13

It was "whom" made me know we are clouds. The first
    distance was difficult, the second—not allowed.

With three piano keys on the Lorquin admiral's wing
    I made a music like a crane asleep. The first note,

unappointed—the second, diffident—the third—not allowed—

5

. . . pencil (re)(ap)pointed was irritated by now . . .

All come without knowing—into what they have come.
    Will be coming to be—a long time.

One found no kindness in words. One said, "I speak your language now—
    okay?" Always they went where they were told.

Magda cried—the German prisoners had new shoes!
    In twelve sugars—well, is it bitter again?

Who isn't washed away is ten rails of blood.
    On eight hooks the flesh of somebody's song.

In four forests, the hero's bowels.

6

. . . and, laughing, Icarus caught the feathers that blew away in the wind . . .

I stepped on Day's snail. What had it done to me?
    Like me, it had eaten, drunk, and loved in its stone shoe.

That day down by the slap lake, her mouth a snail in puff pastry.
    Her thighs—limbs of hunger sprouting leaves

of now. Unappointed in uncut grass—she came—
    she went. Is this what is called a story?

Tongue's an animal could wish a place is gain—is
    such a pretty bird if bushed the summer over.

Trundle in my wooden snail. I mean to conquer—the Garden—

7

    . . . if they look and sigh, I will go with them . . .

The shears of the air are flying. Crying, blind, I stepped
    for three days on snails. My scalp—ploughed up

by the river's roar. Then my son's letter, crumpled morning-glory
    capsized in the cabin window's bindweed-

river-rush reflection. He never loved his wife? Is she to know?
    Always—you must stay with them. Really irritated by now,

like a geranium petted by three rifles. If the peeled-off
    robin red-breasts on the maples turn and sigh,

I'll go with them. This train, where does it go? Please, I speak your language
    now.

8

. . . go to the middle of anything, it is a river . . .

This is none of I—the moon won't bark. Space's kiss, like Sukey's,
    wife off the mark. Whom did you mean me to be? Say it,

space. North of the calendar I'm a train's
    furious slipper. Blow soft—till the fruit's—in the loft.

The pairs, the living rich and fine?
    Divorce is in the water—cataract of train-light,

lungs battling volumes of exotic,
    like the silver wife whom Diller—sold to the miller—

wouldn't have her, so he threw her in the river.

9

. . . bad love is an ass and a few stars . . .

I caught sight of a splendid Muses—night is their over and out.
    I look up: butterfly cut of underpopulated heart.

You cold tonight, honey? I mean you, night,
    you've spent so many nights with me. Like a stuck

gate. Did God dip himself—all that fire—in dust
    and call it love? The moon doesn't need to know

she's in your room—who flows lawlessly in
    from all sides. Why doesn't light

paw at the shell of "whom," a hard case?

. . . what ails the light not alling all the rose . . .

I do not like thee, Doctor Fell, whose pigs are the cook's,
    I know by their looks—married to grease—bedded in gel.

Where's the cloud calamine, soothes the irritation?
    I'm a little dishy, where I am is fishy. I dance for my dears,

who perplex me, who aren't a constant girl.
    Bist du mein? said the apple—to space.

Come sit on the ground, said space—many are already here:
    the sailor who had a red face, the snails,

Berli on the platform blurred by the speed of the train—

Crushed Cargo

(Study #1)

The wind! Forest of frightened women.
Flap of ears sound of wooden castanets panting dry tongues.

(Study #2)

Moleculations. The Little Toe of Their Bacchanal
still unbroken against your house dress
way of feeling alive. The Fruits & Nuts pattern.
Yet you rarely eat among people since in heavenly harmony fully dethinged
they came, the hours, mention of why declined, and went on their way as
prettily as possible, not looking, swiftly easily on their way, their teeth laughing
at the foretaste, more easily killed lying down, imagine the sounds of people
eating together in another room, barbarians.

(Study #3)

The stink of Philomel's nest made him shudder.
He was spanieled. *Bad smell right at the heart of the whole thing.*

(Study #4)

You women are my blue wheels, tiny as the Japanese.
You women, oh you women.
Your mouths purses of crushed leather buttery soft.

                        black mouse–cheese
                        on the dictionary
Consciousness an accidens (is how he spelled it)
The moth of Outside *feeling* through the screen
                    Harley ripping down breast and belly—

        you ride with him, girl, you wear a comb to hold your hair.

(Study #6)

Little finger stuck into the prick–hole in Mapplethorpe's photograph,
do you doubt *hunger be our song* do you doubt *fire in the granary*
do you doubt *hunger for a little while and for that while such hunger*

(Study #7)

I'd be not his *Woman with Pears* but his *Seated Nude, Woman,*
    wouldn't you,
with my hand on my ample or is it your warm underthigh for once.
Lowdown soft then I was a feather then there was confusion but true.

(Study #8)

Men, don't be shy. Sink your naked bodies into a tub of quartered oranges.
Rub. Squeeze.
Is it so bad?

Even Rudy laughs: "Well, I'm certainly swayed."

(Study #9)

        Moonshit in Philomel's nest
the color of Eisenstein's horse (have that painted clean)
hanging by one hoof from a bridge
raised to throw back the rebels.

(Study #10)

The come aches narrowly,
the going is wide.
Who? It. Empty as Stalin's rifle.

(Study #11)

Boiled-cabbage moon of 2 P.M.:
"Friend, I can only stay a moment,
       Dasein is such a guilty——"

(Study #12)

They were

(Study #14)

At the Trocadero I change cars.
Useful if beauty is more than a silhouette.

In my bag, Adam's dried seahorse heart,
which beat only on one side.

(Study #15)

Came down with his axe from the jiltyard.
Came down with his hump
to the stone root ginger this is not your bateau there are several revisions
in the design.

(Study #16)

Breathe on the curtains to see can you make them your own dusty sea.
Stroke the bosom-of-the-garment curves and the fish spines my fingers
smell of, but I thought not.
Breathe on the curtains to see can you.
Don't call me baby if you don't have a life raft.

(Study #13)

Head growing from the end of a twig-brown trunk
to see a going further.

Oh, be excellently seizing.
Calf liver cut out in little stars.

Dangling search needles.
The moon burns that will never be fire.

Le grand tango

You tick like the hot red
Hood of my pickup

One two andthree andfourand
And step on your cigarette

Like a camp of gypsies,
No lo beses en la boca:

And Pussy had them dead on the floor,
Slow slow quick, quick quick slow.

The person who cannot play this game
(Nightbullsnorts   starbreath)

Is the kindling, not the flame.
Questa voglia de amare e di vivere.

I cry unto these hills,
Ills, hear me,

I had her by the ankle,
But she about seen red,

And wouldn't say uncle.

Spangly, the port where you
Empty your pockets, sailor moon.

But the shirt with its arms in the shore
Mud has the longest love.

Que solo e tiempo.
Whoever plays this game

(*Dramático y marcato*)
Is the flame.

A night of falling stars
(*anxieux et presto*)

Is four hours longer than love
(*molto rubato*).

But no love dies all out:
The wings is torn off, is all.

Marina brushes her hair
Like a bandoneon pulled to one side,

Quick-quick slow, quick-quick slow.
Her conspicuous body

Digests a thousand mirrors.
She touches her fingers to Astor's temple

As if love could still be simple.
(*Lento. Meditativo.*)

The flame that climbs the mirror
Is the wound in both dives.

And this one, sleek Santiago,
will do evil to have a part.

With legs called Wrap Around and Serpent,
This one will have a part.

How Can You Hear Me? I Speak from So Far . . .

If my love got up with you in the whirring-
grouse-climb of morning, disheveled
   as Twombly's *Wilder Shores of Love*
(house paint, crayon, pencil, lead),
       would I still be as far from you
as these branches from the evening wine,
  though like oars they fly into it?

I could have been a stick especially picked for whittling,
a whipped leg of cloud, sauntering,
a sweet little bit of stinging,
and gray wolves, I could have been gray wolves
                     let loose on your prairie,
combing the slow fat things from the grass,

but a hole follows me,
a black beetle wanting all the crumb-rain.
I have no other pet.
A kind of loud
when the stairs bang like a shutter.

The dashes I've unraveled . . . dots,
anacoluthons—I never could
    come abreast. Now this rose,
called Breathless, riding in the T-bird convertible
    on my desk, your gift, should I follow,
  these speeds, cutting, streaming,
felt it to be leaving—and I a chair
  strapped upside down on a pickup on I-5,
its black-hooved moose legs
stiffened against the sky.

"To Be Beautiful, the Nose Must Be Straight, and the Eyes Blue"

This superb growth   of Izannah Walker dolls   It'll grass
till the injured ruin it   the rooks too many,
spiders in the hair   oh girls in a little grove
of girls   no woodsman near, no   harvester

Unsubstantiated theory   that the bare feet are "early"
early the troublesome dew   Pretty things!
shush   feel how the earth
moves like a boat   though there is no water

And the candle in the shape   of a fish   utters fire

Maureen Popp, thank you for this charming   exhibit
May your flesh too   be "vibrant as a ripe peach"
far from earth's usage   These little dresses
smother all hunger   Petite ones, with you
I am not to surrender   my eyes   willingly open

see   perfectly friendly

*

I'll forget with you, Heuback Brothers' Chuckling Child
socket head   detachable   as by the red   acts of monsters

Listen to my heart: it's "still   crisp and pretty
and absurd as one could wish"   Like the boy in 12b
a love in wax   and well hung   with beads

"There was surely a companion doll   and one longs
to find her   these arms and legs   may well have been hers"
Torn off   perhaps   in rough play

Fire so pretty   till the injured   lie in it

*

Who put love in my arms   so simply   to hug it
or prop it   to bathe it or bed it   as suits,
till the Jenny heat   lights the skin
till the cradle   in the shape of a fish   utters fire?

Wax   "capable of imitating   a child's
velvety skin"   Cool as Adam's wick
finger   waiting to be lit

          Look, the grass in the boat   is burning
the boat   is burning!   Come out of that transitive
love   you who live   in a fish of flame

Follow my eyes   to somewhere blue

2.

They Liked It Because the Wind Blew, and Blew the Birds About

(a)

~ child, dress in the excited. You could be next. You waterfully, get a sea on.
  You happen. You so already:

~ The spirit of the county, I've seen her. A lizard doing pushups on a rock,
  pulsing with her whole being. Eyeing the coffee grounds of my offering in the
  forest of the south field.
     She's bright as radishes in water.
     Walter, come see the cranes light the swamp.

~ Once it had all to be "taken up" somehow, eye pony stumbling through the
  ding bush.
     I gained the summit and beheld the ample plain below and where the
  village had been the heads of Indian women and children stuck on poles.

         walt!
                 your earwig genitals,
         your bolt that fried the plains.

~ Is there still unusedness here? Half-lung of the wideness breathing?
  A one minute forest in the extra pencil cedar fragrance?

~ Wet Floor signs in the reality-mopped areas.

   The president had a large one, he invited me to blow on it.
   Candle of the birthday of the country.

~ "Death's seeds move in the year," screams packed into mud, dark pounding
every little quality. Sniping starlight, exploded nest of flesh, that one a soldier,
this other to be arranged afterward.
   What makes the meaning (have that meaning
is the size of the Impropriety.
   Showdown at Iron Triangle. " . . . the enemy, thanks to accurate and timely
intelligence. . . ." Go singing. Come to Jesus.
   The dispensary closed at the end of the century.

~ Who took *mi lírica sombra?* Affection is no longer the minute's danger.
Day edged with the vanity of tracks, who often made me cry, come marry and
well our hangdog towns, take us as the wind these trees ("I do get wonderful
action into them don't I").

~ Gray clouds over Idaho, flop on in your unbuckled galoshes.

~ The woolly moon of the sheep, the udder moon of the cow:
   why go back now out of the differences?
   The bobcat hums an umber motion in the snow.
   Climb higher, to Lake Dorothy, rests her oars among the mountains,
      girl bursts of windy mm-hmmms. Today's rose
   hipped, oh why go back now out of the differences?

   Next question.

~ Told you the cow in the meadow, the cow in the meadow, is her song.

~ We had climbed the stairs with longer legs than the English
   on the stage set against an Indian paintbrush sky.

   This American loneliness—tastes right bitter, don't it?
   "I'm goin to have to kill the sumbitch stole my horse."

~ Ferdinand-boatplank to me, whistling with the breath of all the sea birds.
   Who extends me is pearl loosened company, like a beetle
   finding its way into a brilliant day in the prairies;
   for I swear—I was pushed into this country
            by a few staggering sentences.

~ These Burger Kings will never gather
   the hems of the mountains about them.
   Nor an idle Helen,
   sick because the phantom one alone sings and moans in Troy,
   take ship on Lake Powell's pink undersky
   of matter's every-evening desire.

~ Nor will these lion-colored clouds over Salt Lake
   ever taste a Mormon.

~ A fly-sized plane is all the *Om* in Omaha.

~ And Tom Eliot had it all to give away—mountains
   rearing like salmon in his fishing basket.

~ To walk down the center line of a dead-on Nevada highway,
   shaking one's head from side to side!

Jupiter glows over the ice-altar. A hobo spits on his palm.

~ Love, Fear, Anger—the gods
   cruise the Silver Dollar and Jolly Jacks.

~ Come down the road with me, friend,
   like a convoy of the crushed conversations of beer cans.

What Was William Painting?

And I saw the pins removed from the meat and sky.

                              Of the same wish.

And the speechflower, Embraces-everything,

                              wandering in the mists of the manifest.

And the swan-of-a-moment, the I.

                              Singing in its tar pit.

Sweet affection I'll say so, then I'll go.

                              I'll say so. Then I'll go.

Blue be no pretty red apple

                              felt up in a pocket, anonymously.

Blue be standing with me here,

                              not inside like the inside yawn of rain.

Narrative, so happy you're with me.

                              In wet and unkindly years.

But something has me thinking all the time.

                              All the time. Something. Thinking.

Vuggy episode in a '55 Studebaker.

                              jesus I love you.

Twice already leaving, loving from early,

                              and crying from a long way back.

The pearly sluts of snow and streams of brooks,

                              they pass away.

They will be done on earth.

                              Done. As is on earth.

A refrigerator snuff-thunk.

                              Then the sea spills foil,

who would be done on earth—

                              ever rudiment, ever cannon shot.

Then his legs swole up somethin terrible.

                    Clouds. Horses. Skittish and moist.

Away away through the three dot door.

             Through the dot through the three dot door.

A cat licks another cat's face on the bed.

                  Back-lit pink hairy hollyhock ears.

Probably morning,

            a country so long as the sun is interested.

You appetizing, you

              burning point of the shadows.

Love me like a log roughly quoted by the flames.

            Love me roughly now. With your flames.

Yellow petal on William's sleeve—

              a country outside of count:

a coastal hunt and happiness feeling.

                Then what keeps having to be.

Slap dull and it has this memory.

             Slap dull. And it has. Dazed memory.

I felt Twice go into Once, and had had.

             Thrice into Twice, and and and.

What is amounting? Who is having find?

              Not put together plentifully or simply.

From there to here as was as was it was.

              That is not the sound of anything.

Why does Brother Poly press every button?

            Because one might be Throat's Hard Blossom.

One might be Adjustable Speed,

             and one might be Throat's Hard Blossom.

Pink scrotum nailed to the post by older boys.

             Poppies, said the further hills.

What thrill are you looking for?

          Nipple. *That*. The bright metal of success.

And you, all my dying loves, how can I touch
                              the bark of your drowned lemon groves?
Won't you want someone with you there?
                              Someone you know. To be with you there?

The people enter the fabled Land of Tenderness,
                              dressed in different directions.
The judge comes through the olive trees,
                              waist–deep in mist.
Someone asks, "What will be the body?"
                              And he replies, "Water."
Sweet affection I'll say so then I'll go.
                              First a clasp. Then I'll go.

When the Gods Put on Meter

I cleared mother's apartment of her urine-soaked rags today, while she wept.
She wanted to keep them, you see.
She will make more so long as she lives, an hour,

      o loveliest of forms that I may behold you an hour,

      Wife of the Gaze, Husband of the Breath,
      Gleam on the round side of the tear.

          *

A woman is dead in the house across the river.
River of shudders river of quivering grief.

   Hummingbirds who drank from her tower of red,
   know that the Queen of Red River is dead.

   And you, Foss, and you, Tye, cease your squabbling,
   and hear: never again will the beaming Jean

   moon rise over your commingling waters
   and call you her streamers, her troublesome daughters.

   Moping, her pink-haired doll, ape, and deer
   have turned their backs in her vanity mirror—

   who had so little, who would even sing
   to the mouse nesting in her washing machine.

   Only the Alien, propped on the dresser,
   stays as before, its whole being a festered

ear (gods of the beath: is it meter you require?),
feckless in earth's famished, peculiar air.

Oh, never again will the widow Jean open
a window in the Castle Ibuprofen

and float out over dress-ups of snow on
the noble firs of Foss River Grove. In

the morning she thought her husband had spoken.
Now every bone in the darkness is broken.

*

What would you regulate—
        the tiny plenitude of "spontaneous" symbols?
The arrhythmical mass writing of the rain?

                o loveliest of forms

Every bone in the rain is broken

*

You were born in the glade of an averted Eye,
you dressed before the mirror of a hundred arteries—
        oh, don't confuse your arm
with those hanging waters!
        Not *that* leg, the carrot
                            of the downward path!

You learned to desire from where you would never quite be,
        pressed against the flat side of the tear.

*

Where is the rescue?
Cornered children call you River Platte,
your loafshaped covered wagons in their eyes.

Where is the rescue?
Mothers run out to bring in the oxygen
    of the laundry,
shaking themselves into beauty they cannot see.

Do you pick it up, broken-headed animal,
                and blow on its snow-light fur?

I look into the rain barrel of grief
                        and see that it is raining.

*

How frail is our world:

        by day, caramel forests
        lift their green travels. At night,
        quartets of sparks
        fly down to us,
        the coals of the Offering.
        The moon is given
        and taken back:
                as decided.

*

Between labia like the sons and daughters of the same wish,

you have sacrificed in my desire,

Under atmosphere blue as decided,
what is it that lives,
         spine-startled, thrilled by the Flutter-road
of Flies-too-near?

                    *

Ear flushed of its privacies,
                    flushed of its silences,
drawn out to the husband, the Breath,

as Kant walked into Beauty,
forgetting why he opened the door—

"For neither the veil nor the veiled object is the beautiful,
                    but the object in its veil"—

Kant catches fire.

                    *

The rest is the hymn.
What you feel despite the eye is the hymn.

This woman reeking of urine is the hymn.
Jean with her doll-crimped thin dyed hair is the hymn.

                    *

The moist cloud spits the star-seed.
         So begins the sacrifice.
The moon brings the white sheet.

Who accepts breath is sacrifice.
Who sings
            sings worlds frightened and dear.

A Three–Raven Field Talking Dirty Apple Blossoms

And your name, Blue, crouches like a wrestler's head,

Or a voice whose window dismembers the beetle moon.

And your name, Insatiable, stokes a sunflower bonfire

With a voice whose sea is inside out at feeding time.

And your name, Chemical, has no sweet fold et cetera

Nor a voice whose cliffs are anybody's heart.

And your name, Leaves a Light on in the Void,

Clicks in the all–night stapler of your theater.

And your name, They Had Doubt, slews in a Cloud Magellan

With a voice whose Mary is two blues from origin.

And your name, Halfer, *ignora la otra mitad,*

Whose voice piles weapons in the pick–up beds of exile.

And your name, Curled Flame, licks the matchbook of the cause,

Like a voice whose Rome pisses through every little animal.

Number, I Call You, Though You Bear No Name

May I see the water's water. After cottontail light,
   three drunks on the sill of, suppurating white
dawns on the should of, may I come out

the light? This tall surf wants what god wants,
   to walk smoking over blue
hearts. *I got no splendor, baby.*

We are wet, world, wet in your turbulent
   rhythms three. And love, dive-spiraling apple peel,
knifed by too many breaths. And the hologram

Jerusalem of the mind now gibberish gut blow
   to Euclid vortical nonlinear dot come dark.
I've seen the cut of your arts in the cougar-baiters'

alder chapel of butchered beef (roll in your hand,
   you Jesus-likes, the knife of stinks, and weep);
seen it repeated in the swift chops

of the asylum's hands as the patients jumped
   juicy funny little next, naked sudden feet and all for why,
while nurses paraded the starched

charts of doses and decimals . . .
   Who but a child could climb inside
the molecular waters, here like a whiter ship?

O birds that crop the skies, shrill delibles,
   I detest the thing with wings won't fly, Godfire-
unmoved-thing, no jar of fireweed honey

what's so sweet. Our Dove's a fat man's tits
   plovering a T-shirt; our dancer, halt, jump-in, Oedipus,
his bad foot. I don't like my heart, its momenta,

red pulls, operators, eigenaches, bursts
   of quick and *done*   quick and *done*   quick and *done*.
But we will own what is ours. You who shoot craps

in the casinos of raving faces, were you anywhere
   father when Holocene entered, sat, licked
her rat tail? Or were you puzzled—

monstered, monster—by your handiwork? She's beautiful.
   It is necessary to say that. Beautiful
her blood of a certain color.

Pasting Nothing in the Wound

I won't have you hiding in the ground mist.
You were in my bed, around me like a cock ring.
Do you think a piece of cold-cut on the barbwire

is farewell? Do you think these floating posts
are memories of elevation?
I's I can paste in my little book?

What you gave me was only the violin
of a little Monday, the first bar of the wound.
The height you left me I could powder

like an aspirin under a spoon, avalanche
of gag and sour, grimace lyric and anodyne.
I would be all the second line I cannot remember,

if a firm terrible hindering hadn't seized my mind,
lying as I did a moment too long
in the wide circle of your—was it arms?

Was I so little to you that you wiped your musics
off my tongue? Was I back singer and robber
description, laborer and alley clatter,

stinks and disappearing tails? I was *that* close
to the rattle of the great harvest of love.
A meadow king. A child. If it's keepaway

you're playing, you win. I don't even remember you,
though I have a feeling about you . . . and a name
for you: Pastes Nothing in the Wound.

Nice little <u>a</u>, your pearly tiles

Sing to me, had a horse, had a—
oh, to feel it for a minute coming faster.

When the circus flaps, the kindness of smelling!
Be my elephant, *a*, and I'll ride
with a higher tush than the English.

I have nothing, you cry, *but what you gave me*
by hopping a thunder. Oh, *a*,

do you think you meant well?

The cross swells and froths, we know it arisen.
The teat swells; foams:
    meadow of the damned.
Ignorant residue, the lip
collects the dead.

Still you're big at night when the stars
are bright, over the turkeys, the sheep,
and the orange trees.

Ah, I have a meat heart
I long to love you for.

If you were kind you'd be
a guide to left over,
        and neck, and ten
    little ways of calling
a man too numerous to compose a vowel.

Arrogant rider, don't be unsociable.
Torch the rigid woods.

Take Me to the Godfish

Roaring clover.
In my torso of stars, I killed it.
Ravaged it, like a white-torn river.
I couldn't breathe, so I killed it.
I was excited, I couldn't breathe.
Standing up like the hair on your darker than anything.

    Came to be rosy not to be careful,
    came to be quickly came to be stopped.

To know this thing was in me, they sold maps to my grounds.
Squeezed-down Jack thing had not come all the way.
While they talked freak look out it bites I feasted.
I said flagellum they said we feel some concern.
You were told weren't you no no one said a word.
How many ounces of poison go into a Symposium.

Hauled ass in my Unimog.
Hacked the snooping moon from the side mirror.
Shot the Strip back into desert dark.
Gave some Arkansas children matches you all have a nice day.
Killed three sexaphones, the holes of each, complete.
The heart of father's fly—whacked that. It was sweet.
Killed kiss and worry, and her bloodied lip.
I was eight California condors tearing up her bedclothes.
Gassed the zoos. Virused the environmentalists.
Played *you began* on a cockroach-colored violin.
Oh who remembers what I was any how I began?
Looked for the address all morning, laughing and talking.
Wretch. Wretch.

Modern Love

Tonight the clouds lie belly up. The moon
slips among them, quick

about something. Your hand, a cold
blue iris, blooms late

from an early snow. Touch me
and I am ice scraped from the windshield of a car

in which Nagasaki once tore off
its burning face. It is horror, these moist jammed

repetitions, red tongue
shooting up like a poison mushroom

in the drizzle of the other's kiss.
The history of nightmares has yet to be written . . .

Tonight we are Benjamin arrived at the border,
sans nationalité: "Dear Adorno, I will

the tattoo artists' pattern sheet to the rain."
Nothing remains but what is white and puckered

like skin when a bandage is removed: we sleep
on that mattress. Where were the mothering

elements when I stifled the rabbits of your breathing,
mouth to mouth, on the killing fields of mash

and desire? Swarms of antlers
cross the moon of your flesh, velvet

stroking the goddess of the arrow . . .
In a Russian hat of gray fur,

morning will find us curled beside the graves
we dug, without the strength to roll ourselves in.

Oh, to climb into a passing
coal train while the guards light cigarettes,

to lie there endlessly,
listening to the rhythm of the wheels.

Roaring Clover

A wood below a cloud is—do this for me.
Twisted knee immensity. Want to play?

When I'm the maker and not under God—
yellow urine in the snow,

so hot you never did that, get back
in the car—I'll be once and not,

such an aroused Feeling. Mean-

while my rose basin
bursts with machines. *Wast called*

a transgressor from the tomb.
And your smile, dear—agates

sacked in cheesecloth. Want to play?

My *femme du punition,*
I'll be your alibi—the way six women go

from house to house, patting everything,
space is so nicely folded:

the homeowners not offering a taste
of the cricket sauce—they're in.

3.

A Short Ailment. Appointed with a Swarm, Massy, Low

The eye is *fled* that does not paint what happened, wrecks of lack stuff.

O moon, punched out of the tall celery palms of L.A.,
        stop a while. Chew. I love you, I really love you.

I had a threatened. Was several times a pupil of close over me.

To Adam: heaps of cocks. then the hay is carted.

To the cow whopped by an oar of the sun: out at sea, wet and
        wildly wide, *the big burn.*

With the missus up in the flowingly written. That was the breath
        of the black paper.

To Thelma: I looked for you in the rattlesnake colors of Grand
        Coulee. Found your hat, a square piece of turf.

On Thelma's laugh: a pitcher never drowns, it Aprils.

Dull pops of reminiscence. Didn't we mean for you to hear us? Forgive us. The
        grasshoppers had more fire.

Once she would have buzzed us in her yellow Piper Cub.

Adulterous time, when to another's bed thou creepest, thighs
        thrashing like feeding fish . . .

To the yellow-headed blackbirds perched on marsh reeds by Highway 2:
        such a dear noise. Go to Thelma.

Something in my eyes. I would not say universal, but wet, a dark field.

Not Shallow Smaller but a Larger Flickering

A death, a death is not a goodbye, not shallow smaller but a larger flickering.

Regret makes a way walled if it is already grieving.

Chill and shudder is how I know the other version is right:
   the Child was born of the vine's root,
       nursling torn, inlined with ruddy hurry,
           pushed up and out
               in a thousand tendrils.
Spring water had reached
              down the pants of the furrow
   and tickled—and lingered—

   oh, careless, here they come already,
       the maenad and the satyr,
   swinging the cradle between them.

"I give my tongue to the dogs."

~

For seven years my brother brushed the ants, the eager dark, off his heart.
The cancers drank him like red wine
and the clouds passed away that were the all-night whites of his eyes.

Why any cut is a demander, when there are ordinary orders going on,
   when there is daily if not entirely,
was why I was angry;

      and the hornet flying the next morning in the stopped-up car
      was the dead living among the living

13 hours unwilling, yet willing   bewildered,
                    don't you think so?

                        ~

I will not believe in Dionysus this year, though I sought out *zoë*,
to whom I spoke reasonably—not fireless,
                    I held a leaf in my hand, a green match, to find her.
No, why should I lie? I struck her, I am not a good man.

"The fortune of excrement that escorts us like a lamp,"
            this is how I know it—
the smell of his emptying shit-bag,
            as of something dying to be gone,
            his inventions, songs, schemes to get rich, broken record

    deals, wit all come to this heartless brown,
this is how I know the hunt was already raging when the Child was born.
                I mean to be *so* dried
                when I get back and breathe when I can.

                        ~

Perhaps our mother, a "raving woman,"
            got inside him, he broke everything, nightly broke open
a sea of Caribbean rum,
                    went to bed gang-hooked by dawn,
his bowels not all baby, explain horror, not all well.

Women loved him, the horned infant,
his voice tortured the darkened faces in the clubs
with the heat and sky and storm of its beauty,
                    the reared belly of its longing.
        Some are careless in their desires

and pass away early

              (I wish anger   I wish matches)

leaving themselves all over the day,

         for he offered you sounds of every kind,
            whirring plumage,
            the croaking of tree-frog masks,

and the screams he crutched to the bathroom
      will not go back to bed.

       ~

A wide leaving is a strange move, no grounds for a footed feeling.
The only lady who'd been sawed in half and lived to the height of five roads
      is the hot water bottle
of my northwest bed
between the coughs and rusted blood
of the train worming back from Mexico.
  I mean to be dry when I'm attractive again, and the shit and the blood

                    are pooled in a little sentence.

I wish a great darkness on the vines, unseasonable snow—
wide,
    a covered piano,

     or else *Blood and fire and dust will mix*
  (clear, that last tear from under his eyelid was clear)
and at my bidding everything you see will come alive.

Kid, fallen into the milk, cared for by his divine nurses,

and I hefted what was left of him into the Harbor General ER,
                              where the too-fresh intern
            —the naked boy rode away on the he-goat—
was slow to grant him morphine,

                now the time has come, now the flowers are here.

In Elgar's concerto, Jacqueline du Pré
        almost expires for a moment
        in the long rotting resonance of her cello—
                        a dark brown sound.
Did she crawl into her instrument
        to get to the tree from the fruit?
                To the darkness
                        brightness requires?

        Some who are crushed do not go all the way.
        A bit of wind a ball of bees and they are humming.

Nothing helps. He was careless. He went everywhere.

The Day Is Extreme When There Is No Frame

Massive growths in the tumors, the liver
a sea of Leviathans. Space has identified you,
you can be cornered now, in every corner
of the sea. Your new straw hat with the brown
satin band and splash of white orchids
lies on the dresser in the dawn-dark
as on a rocky shore. Wake, my love,
break the faint snore that starts and stops
like a motor that won't catch
somewhere out at sea, take up your hat,
in which you were young again yesterday,
your blue eyes so beautiful, and wave it
at the violence of the morning.

Rust with Night and Language in the Waste

What part of time have you to give? Your little bit
                 of arrangement
marrow credit *concetti*, how much room can there
be in a noun? Give them the due distress of your mind,
your come to tears, face down.

Had you plenty of in, time's not-melt, what would you give them
                 more than these orange ruffle-mouthed
be well gladiolas, rackgasps laid on the grass,
choked in waveless light? What part of love
have you to give now they resemble

nothing nor grammar nor face in the black window
                 floating over the kitchen sink,
who never had plenty of in where all that falls
                 falls the same way,
and goes away? And what is position if many go on,
                 a narrative they will go,
to windows apple rain required?

Loves, I have spoken to your graves—I have explained,
                 lie back, I have explained
I can do nothing.
                 A come to tears face down wet woods leaves
against the mouth,
                 and averaging,

leaves and averaging, a due distress is my mind.
                 A noun
                 is an offering. A verb—
a verb is hard rain.

I'm Cooked, I'm Beefsteak Letting Go of the Grass's Tail

I was not born to scatter seed on Pluto's mattress
was I now
but I tire of the earth
stink of daylight.

I held my sick wife like a washbowl of water
   filled to the brim I held her   —
by nature a spoiler,
               but wishing to be reasonable.

                  If she were still in that lake
                  of afternoon light on the bed—

Her blond wig, Rover,
last pup of Thunder,
   sleep, sleek perky pekinese tail
        blood wig
on the
slept on the pink-tiled
bathroom counter.

I sulked in the orange Polaroid glare of her
   / lethargy I am sulfury
in the orange Polaroid glare of what I

               didn't I wish to be reasonable?

Sun up and the earth's all over me again.
    A lava glow

heats the blinds. Already a fly,
      smallengine whine of winged garbage,
      bangs its head against the window.

Come back, darkness, am I the hateful?
Take me to the spilled one / it isn't far.

Cup of Astonishment and Desolation

The sea, here,
purples and silvers, happy dishtowel
eve. I could be all a believer longer
       if I and my night-shy
       pansy company
                    (*his graves are about him*)
had waited to take the uncut mild,
                    who took instead the meat
(my mouth was opened, the city smitten). The pen
       spits like a hotter water.

The current-lines in old window glass
       are fragile as Apollo's quotation marks,
flawed out of the vulvocracy
              and thou shalt surely die.
   Look through them as the dolphin
       moon falls backwards into sea rocks,
and still your blood
                    will be upon everything.

In the sixtieth year and ninth month of my captivity,
   I say to what has not yet burned in the fire,
                         Go, hide thee,
while I write *And it came to pass.*

These deck doors swing open like the breath in matches.

Person Throwing a Stone at a Bird

A white screaming hurting anything
sloshes sour milk sound on love's
        Dead Cow Meadow.
Beak's strafe-screech of *ee's*,
          whistleblast eruptions of bony I'm me's.

Fiery ringlets today in the sky's hair salon,
and I a mountain perspiring in its furs—
the early crab
        belly light gone.

O kill me if you must, world of be-
around, but today, please,
a beach with no dead.

Even this abyss is your child.

4.

You Should See the Letters I Would Have Written
If They Hadn't Agreed to Everything

O Sea face, the way you curl up
as you approach,
    like a dog hit on the road
and rising on its front legs to greet its master,
    seems natural and necessary to me.
I will never. Stall. *Of course you miss*
    all that stormy identification, boy,
but it still lines your slicker mind,
    and the bird is anyhow a branch
of the branch, as flames
    are branches of the burning tree.
The forest antlers the stag;
    the veined white, the aster.
She trembles. This ferocity—the vein
    in her forehead antlers a strong summer.
"An earth wide moth is something,"
    but the glacier lily heats
a tube house in the snow, wasps
    dropping down on her yellow hair.
Rain!—
    The gondoliers cover their boats.
Rise Icarus, cast-eyed pigeon,
    from your frantic circlings in the Grand Canal.
Be again the air's branch. Rise,
    veined hand, and calm her face.
I will never leave a lover who drives through rain
    just by being beautiful.
I will never. The positivity of that.

The Outside Butterflies Are Trying to Join the Inside Butterflies

O girls, girls, girls of little-piggy-
went-to-market toes, why wouldn't I
understand you—aren't we all of mothers
born? I, too, know minutes like a cat-

fish gasping in a boat with nobody in it,
and they call that the soul. O girls!
Dream-heavy, your bush dips like a brush
in the lake's nasturtium afterglow.

The trees on the shores stand stiff:
lashes unable to meet and latch
like the brass catches on an antique bible,
to force you face down

into revelation. Scarlet lake
up to your thighs, you wake
and scramble from the wet canvas,
o girls of the toes that cry

all the way home, girls in your snarled
veil of midges. I say: Stand back
from the deeper pigments. It's true
men don't know how to love you. They think

you're really something and only pretend
to be nothing, like wallpaper pattern
hard to see in the glare of the sun. They think
they are the sun. They fear dark matter.

Facades are what they like, painted faces.
But girls of faraway home and none,
don't let anything take you in.
There is no in. Even when your skin's

covered with wet mouths, there is no in.
A boat on the lake is as "in"
as in is. Pick up an oar, do it.
Now the other one. O girls,

the slender eyelash of an oar!

Insatiability

For every angel
                    a preposition.
You call,
            swarm guitar string longitudes,
o air flame shining relations
                        wandering contemporary.

    Steeple white clapboard "to"
                spikes enormity Iowa blue—
as the moon is a clasp for night.

  "Of," "with"—moments like rain,
when what rises from the river   is not only river.

Lightning never lay me bare to bed.

    She sat atop him as if he were everything,
    but not to her—

tablespoon of sugar in water.

Spaces be cream
            or exaggerated like raspberries, red hustlers.

        Roots that tug to be "up,"
        "inside,"
            will never find a bride.

We're oyster spit, yet the sea
opens before us the white swan of the wound.

Till I Can Face Again the <u>Cracked Open</u> of Another Morning's Flaunted Wings

You had to be
all this rage, stars crowding the hole
in your copyright page? Had to smell
of quantum foam, its pulp and revel?
What you are you are.
I'm talking to you just to be civil.

Nothing can hold you but the space you hold.
Book of the Boar. Book of the Avant Garde.
Still, you're no made-a-day rainy-day window
wiper pen, only-snow-expected sequel:
who but you is the trillium's
blunder in the charger blue?
Book of Gardening, Book of the Law.

All the rest is more mind and winter,
no way to chase a darkness with silver.

The flaw is matter doesn't know one
but is one, but desires to remain the other.
Bother, your two-sided love for me
and every other. Yet as birds
blunder in the charger blue,
wisely you rise in us but a little way—

enormous openings beset by clouds.

Romanza

As the pink inside a horse's lip
falls from the brown spots like a water-
fall from the raised-up dirt of things,

our lady of appropriations
lifts clouds from the horizon,
   stuffing them into her bag of comparisons,
        as Proust

filched Whistler's glove at a reception
        (some take what they like to be
        not too distant).

Thesis 5: self is, I don't know—pick-up sticks.

Thesis 6: self is importantly alive.

———————————

   Passion's seed lay on the dirt, thinking
about having sex but wanting maybe this once
        to levitate, instead,
unless that's the sign of a "romantic complex."

Oh "break him and shatter him and whatever-it-is
will whatever-it-does to him still."

Thesis 2: the "interests of the future" are now.

So stars are prefaces, and the blacker they are,
the prefacer

(additional material
stored in a safe place).

Rink organ music burbles,

                            makes big
              welcome
half the starry night.

Space is no shortcoming, or why would it?

Sway, my love. Now inside, now outside, edge.

—————————

    Our lady circles the idea of an April ago
as June
circles a dead pelican
in its into-the-rocking-song-commended boat.

She says, "The roses you sent me, Philosophy,
              arrived too late.
Now I shear dahlias of breath from the sea whine"—

           philosophy's smell still lingering in her hair.

—————————

The snipe's
four bent soda-straw legs
straddle the sand's liquor.
So then, she sees, one can be both here and there,

like the sea undoing her green braids.

"I'll shear oceans of delphiniums for my sisters,
the women of thesis 12, their eyes
the shallow lakes on long oars."

———————————

If a certain lady and a certain gentleman (make this brief)
        ignore each other on the beach

        —I see the hydra flutterings of her skirt—
            (for pity's sake, be quick)

never to meet again except as black clouds meet

        —how stirring they are, these breathing commotions—

let no one prevent them from drinking deeply of their grief.
What is feeling that you can throw it away so cheaply?

Thesis 20: no one should leave anybody, except unhappily.

———————————

But I don't want to be
in one place only,
nor am I, swinging
north and south,
plus you can twist the seat about plus to close your eyes
is nervous and thrilling.

Pick a green worm off a tomato plant if this be living.

In this way pleasures pool
        between accidental narrative rains.

The wind plucks at the gentleman's trousers. His legs are double-bass strings.

_____

Thesis 33: color, if never folded together at the ends
and offered to a lover's mouth, like breath with mayonnaise,
is still color.

Really it's the stars and not us that look tiny.

Stand up on your skates, Love. Rise in my estimation.

The Violin of a Little Monday

You're the ripped
slumber of a hardwood tree, stick
is the size of a Horace at these speeds to stay,
as noon is two bars longer than evening, the
hive that eats its own honey. The eagle in you
climbs,   corrects.   (We were
almost happy,
weren't we—
it was none of these, earrings in a milk-
glass   jar.) Yes, tall so soon, dune of vibra-
tions, merely and large, you the sky
assault silverly.
                """"Shivered by your
candor, the hand
spates till ample speaks special
and the triangle's worried. I can be
rough inclined, you say,   or
painstaking squeaky. Then be so
with the late sun
coming in.
                Quick,
                say
                it:
                the
                am-
                ber
                light
                is
                coming
                in

Open Violin Case

Tell me a score I should meet at the back of my hair,
up there to the left come surprise,
scooped from a melon of everything
like a moon of toothsome water.

Must I grieve to the hoe's *chud chud*
(for seed I am would not be spat out ever)?
Oh, shut up, you did bitter better
in your runaway heavy breathing

hurt feelings. Now you're like the sea-
blue plush of an empty violin case
splayed open on a chair, while beyond the three
misshapen notes of blackbirds on the balustrade,

bathers char on the sand by a sea
so long able it goes with the sky
as Victorian plots go with upholstered chairs.
How bow the waves that in the distance cry

all together, we can hum
only if we hum all together?
(Kneels the violin on the air,
giving away its animal

Icarus in Daedalus's Studio

A wing's a bridge
                    made of light and lightness.
Such an unattaching, then *then*, such a humming garden.

What is finished is brutal. Pink
            swallow, brown wings and tail
                        acock on a porcelain vase,
can be diving so,
only if whole is the greenest color.
                        Return, world.
Be a little whether.

                    So the boy sees the caterpillar
Wing ache a rise from the artificer's leaf
            and with his hand steadies his plenty
(I cannot see
what I shall),
            as his genitals, two hummingbirds,
                    sleep beak to tail,
gentle, not as the seed was written.

Zucchini-nosed, the youth twigs,
            past the girls in their headbands at the well,
    past *shapes are there*, past a reason given,
how the line of the rise is the garden in the fountain,
            blue the displacement of the sign.
                (I can think of so much,
go around and around in a minute, lips open.)

Calamity's crack—is feather's—very heaven.
    What heights are eager?

Child, it's you who thirst,
you who will water your wings in shouting air.

Yes,
we were pleased with the order,
the cloud-fruit the corn-sun and everything too big.

Every Color Is a Wolf

> they   howl
>   chasm - watered:

pad-crunch:
color runs over the eyes' snow.

    What is living our life?

Every color is a wolf, furred island of hunger.
She will not be denied the exacting birth.

Listen to cedar's tawny scarlet
   under thunder so rapidly.
Lilac also has it all the way,
      not short as a faithful dog
      running beside the sweated horse of *whose song*
      like the color of moonlight in whiskey.
Orange has no notch for stopping,
   you've seen that. A broken-open yellow is sunset,
      need I say why there are roads?
Pink: actual.
Pansy face belly shattered velvet silly.

Earth, the Detail.
The light's silken bristles.

You accepted the bracelet worn by the sun it rusted?
Ah go on.

At the foot of Niagara Falls, pulverized light.
Oh but sometimes I be red, I scooter red on comma wheels
   down the driveway of flame and light.

Hip-hop bearings & whirrings   so fine!

You suppose you know why I want—intrusion?
Antagonistic—pleasures? Because my soul is gray?
      I say, rain has the right abandon,
        take the blows of its green-tipped hair.

Yet she remains, pale Eurydice, in his harmonies
      if not his melodies,
           as Beethoven's "Kyrie"
              turned up greasy,
          jacketing the pantry butter.

Yes, always she is there, moan and la,
   song blue-bludgeoned in shiver emerald shade.
Shade is the sent away of same,
   and who is from sent away is low,
     brown as in dirty turquoise
                  or rocky shore cocoa ocean foam
     (hold in your hand this heart
     of crawling iridescence, and blow).

But the Detail! Need I say why there are roads?

Green light on the buoy, red on the tanker's stern.

How can we be all ours a whole?
Low over Gold Bar, a yellow moon
      hooks the town steeple on its horn.

"All around the world poured out colors, constantly new, pink clouds gathered
in violet cumuli which unleashed gilded lightning . . . mosses and ferns grew
green in the valleys. . . . This was finally the setting worthy of Ayl's beauty. . . .
   'Ayl! Come outside with me. If you only knew . . . Outside . . .'
   'I don't like it, outside. . . . All that confusion has come.'"

Ah, go on. What is hardy
   colors any soil,
     as asparagus exclaims in hot water.
Wear that tigereye on your ear,
   the light will like your noise.
Oh be laughing. Oh go on.

No. 2 Pencil Quaquaversal Shout

Cut it out.
Quit that.
Out of that.
Shout stout out.

I said, Quit that. Out, stout. Quit that. Cut it out.
Stout's in a hood. Stout's no good. Colored's whited out. Understood?

Who put the blue in the colored well. Well who. can't figure that out?
Who put the bell on the colored cat. Well ring well shout, get on with that.
Colored in the well. Othered. Bothered. Smothered in the well. Well in.
   Well well.
Well hell. Hell's bells. Well hell.

Make a woman of me would you white? White me would you? Dominate out.
June, june, shout frank out. Stout frank, stop. Let june out.
Did I didn't I did I didn't I hear her moan?
Bloom, june. Bloom a bloom a bloom. Pencil get busy. Draw june from home.
Quit quarrel. Quash qualm. Rout stout. Stout get out.
Tree's in the water water's in the tree. That's the way it ought to be.

Who put the colored in the white well tangle.
Colored put the angle in the blue black tango.
Pencil put the wrangle in the blue black mangle.
Pencil put the pussy in, pencil get the pussy out.

Tango me, june. Tango me, frank. Tango me out of this lonely place.

Two pink sunrises dulled by ice. One for the cats. One for the mice.
Find the cat. Where's the cat? Cat's in the well. Mouse is in the cat.

June, june, tango frank out. Frank, tango june out of this lonely race.

Tree over the river. Emerald pool. No. 2 pencil shades it cool.
Get on with the shout. Stomp stout out.
Acquire that quire. Quaquaversal shout.
Plural transversal. Bloomabloomabloom.

I air with irises. Tango's boss. Twenty-five dimensions, none of them lost.
Me into them. Them into you. Green into brown into black into blue.

Boom boom. Boom ba boom. Boom boom. Boom ba boom.

Quit that.

Boom ba boom.

Quit that.

Boom.

Quit that.

Ba.

Cut it out.

Venus Rolling Up Her Stockings because of Much Memory

Deep wader all electron, no wing & verge—
like a bug upside down on twanging ground,
spinning fast—I say get up now and see

the well in the welcome and good yellows
breaking from the orchard. I say a leaf
stretches very much stream as I am tall.

What is just about lemon spray in the face
of every wanting is very climate,
it is, as any sneeze of the wind might blow you

into the capital of Keats and Rome,
where brown is a rich color for marketing.
No spider will quit today to gather

ocean Helen's spoken take-aways. Minutes,
our magi, come and go in a minute,
these their fleas and randoms, blue rootage,

and lightning lattices. If I am king
of anything, bring it to me: I will exchange
its war bonds for—oh, sing to each other,

all you originals, as roofs are passed
among snowflakes, the handouts of a different
kingdom. Punching up its bored hair,

the evening would like to be held by the
wandering circle around it, masterpiece
that shines and darkens and is really no

trouble. But is this the use of the spread?
Philosophy is dead! Look down: crackleware
arrangements, the big questions farmed into fields,

so much permission, and no bloom in the
labeling. "Oh, you do, you're so hyacinth."
How kind. Who said that? Was it you, veiled Mul-

tiple—the one they call *beautiful noise?*

Clouds of Willing Seen in the Bird Day

Amiable Monet, in lieu of *that*, had a *now*
        postdated like his eyes—
                crafty, a beaver's,
      flush with the floating waterlily fields.

And you: anybody more remote would be dead
                        languaged,
    you are nice library, nice library, sit.

Who hasn't been out of line for a long time,
   like the cooked-spinach-green boat in *Sunrise*,
     twenty feet short of the

wobble laid down by the orange sun
             low in the emerald air of the sea?
   (it's so easy to difference and cumber
   (an eyelet passed through to a little evil
   (boomerang of heartbone
         winging into the dark refusal of beauty.

What is special electrical railroad in anyone
             that anyone should feel so wide
open under the moon's sudden cheekbones?

Scatter corn on the dock
   as the wild geese breast toward you on the languid lake
   their greeny-platinum circles of evening.

What you cannot think will be your life.

Taller by the Non-Thinglike

He says it snows in Italy and Iowa,
Like the morning after sex. He says
Following the land very nearly
All of it at once. May be having
Earth. Chickens I'm blest if I can.
The pieces widen. To be let down again
At the knees. Go, idiot eye in the wheat,
A dog day to have
Strongly loving repeating being.
                        The sal-
Vadordalliance of my dreams
Melts a skinned rabbit over form,
But my words
              practice tiny displacements
Like everything that would accomplish
The messianic world.
                        Yesterday
Speaks of himself again, so as to acquire
Self-acquaintance, as five I's
Are V if a painting is a picture
Every inch. But today fits a little not,
Supposing curlily.
    It is not the Sea—
The Woman Pouring Milk, the Woman
Drying Her Feet, The Geographer,
The Astronomer, The Slick Sloppy
Settlement of Claims. Unrecuperated surplus
  Is a woman I know, I work at a bar
In the Vale of Tempe, after that
I was instructed and everything.

I had a coat made for her. It did not
Fit her well. Now she goes naked.
She keeps touching her hair.
She says she is a happy woman.

Feather's Wives Are All Good-Looking

Flute, flute, this is a change.
The news? A tiny bit of flutter. Up
on the stalk the bleeding heart

utters out-of-beds; the whole garden
dips and behaves.

And should I pony to little bed?
HORSE me to the table, morning, like a winning cake.
Daylight
has laps of breath for us,
legs for us,   morning (gate) has legs for us
who would not pony to little bed.

Why which, then, without difference when?
Why pearl without lily elaboration?

Cow lie down, horse be our baby blues,
horse be our column of wasps.

Flute, o
peculiar new kneeler on the air! Any
bottoming by breath's early light,
virile butte carved clear,
is feather weight to you

who would not pony to little bed. So:

feather my bench, feather the weather.
Feather. Feather. Feather. Feather.

Paths Jack Philosophy strews with jumbo jacks for us,
the little train in the mouth that stops and goes for us,
the vanilla of 7 A.M., the cinnamon of noon,
will get us there,
as the moon in the sky
is a blossom in the water.

Out the window of outside-phenomena,
one leg out, one leg ahead,
would not pony to little bed.

Here's a Development

Let a line muse, go line.
As in wader notnumber, notnumber
not repeating tall titled.
Frog noises, these avocado testicles,
everything bronzed in a late-colored hum.

Is that you in the fortieth window of the poem?
A good spot (they're all good spots).
But the rose is
            mouth   lift   equitable

mimicry of the late-colored cloud.
The mouth is one ahead;
                   here's
a development.

A little shadow invents go fly.
You flap, my love, like a ladder in a sunset of champagne.
Your orange fingernails are pink in a later world.

How can *it* be a little more than *that*?
The moon strips like an alder to bathe:
      maybe you became a fish.
The jungles of 'Nam march on Spokane:
      maybe you became a mist.
The ivy-light covers the mirror:
      maybe you became a leaf of fog.

Leaf of fog leaf of fog leaf of fog.

I've seen you when your particles waded.

I greet your help and hero hum.

Notes

The title *The Violence of the Morning* is adapted from the title of Jack Yeats's painting *The Violence of the Dawn*.

The title "Minotaur Provides for This Paragraph" is adapted from a note at the end of Georges Bataille's *The Inner Experience*. (For a review that he started in 1933, Bataille proposed, but did not use, the title *Minotaure*.) The notes of *Inner Experience* also contain the model for the bracketed editorial material in the poem.

    The verse cited in the poem is from Golding's translation of Ovid's *Metamorphoses*.

In "Jove's Thunder But a Murmur in the Leaves," the line on Dionysus is from Nietzsche, the line on dolphins from St. John Perse.

In "Go to the Middle of Anything, It Is a River," the material on the Windemere Retention Camp is adapted from Sarah Moskovitz's book *Love Despite Hate: Child Survivors of the Holocaust and Their Adult Lives*.

"Le grand tango" is the name of a composition by Astor Piazzolla. The italicized lines are indebted to him.

The title "How Can You Hear Me? I Speak from So Far . . ." is from René Char.

The statement "To be beautiful, the nose must be straight, and the eyes blue" is from a book on antique dolls. The poem is dedicated to my cousin Robert Young and his wife, Iva Dell, doll maker.

The title "They Liked It Because the Wind Blew, and Blew the Birds About" is from Gertrude Stein. *"Mi lírica sombra"* is from Federico García Lorca.

"What Was William Painting?" is dedicated to William Brice. "What will be the body?" re-echoes a passage in the *Upanishads*.

The phrase "When the Gods Put on Meter" is from the *Upanishads*. This poem is dedicated to Jean Smith.

In "Roaring Clover," the quotation "Wast called a transgressor from the womb" is from Isaiah.

"Take Me to the Goldfish" is dedicated to Toni Ellen Hakinaw.

"A Short Ailment. Appointed with a Swarm, Massy, Low" is in memory of my aunt, Thelma Faught Myrick, the only heroine of my childhood.

The italicized phrases in "Not Shallow Smaller but a Larger Flickering" are adapted from translations of ancient Greek in Carl Kerényi's book *Dionysos: Archetypal Image of Indestructive Life*. The poem is in memory of my brother, Jack Raymond Bedient.

The title "Cup of Astonishment and Desolation" is from Ezekiel. A few of the phrases derive from the same book. The term "vulvocracy" is taken from Nietzsche.

"Person Throwing a Stone at a Bird" is the title of a Paul Klee painting in the Museum of Modern Art, New York.

The sentence "you should see the letters I would have written if they hadn't agreed to everything" is from Jack Yeats's writings. "An earth wide moth is something" is from Gertrude Stein's.

The title "The Outside Butterflies Are Trying to Join the Inside Butterflies" is adapted from André Breton. This poem is for Kappy Wells.

"Till I Can Face Again the *Cracked Open* of Another Morning's Flaunted Wings" was suggested by Paul Klee's painting of a huge open book (a gaping hole in its middle) suspended in the starry night. The last line is adapted from René Char.

"Romanza": the clause "break him and shatter him and whatever–it–is will whatever–it–does to him still" is from Jack Yeats.

"Open Violin Case" is loosely patterned after Matisse's painting by the same title in the Museum of Modern Art, New York. The poem is for Molly and Robert Reidelberger.

"Icarus in Daedalus's Studio" was suggested by an antique bas-relief in the Villa Albani in Rome. (*The New Larousse Encyclopedia of Mythology* contains a photograph of it.) The poem is dedicated to Sara and Carl Monser.

The prose at the end of "Every Color Is a Wolf" is from Italo Calvino's *Cosmicomics*.

"Venus Rolling Up Her Stockings because of Much Memory": in Balzac's story "The Unknown Masterpiece," the river-christened courtesan Catherine Lescault is the subject of the painting *La Belle Noiseuse*. In his book *Genesis*, Michel Serres remarks of this painting, "I think I know who . . . the querulous beauty [is]" and adds: "Noise is metaphysical" and again: "Noise cannot be a phenomenon; every phenomenon is separated from it, . . . as every message, every cry, every call, every signal must be separated from the hubbub that occupies silence, in order to be, to be perceived."

The phrase "clouds of willing seen in the bird day" is from Gertrude Stein.

~

This collection is dedicated to the memory of Vanessa Stribling Bedient.

Acknowledgments

Often in somewhat different form, the following poems appeared in the journals specified:

In *New American Writing*, "Was It Stella, or Was It Stella?" and "Number, I Call You, Though You Bear No Name"; in *Fence*, "Go to the Middle of Anything, It Is a River" and "Minotaur Provides for This Paragraph"; in *Agni*, "To Be Beautiful, the Nose Must Be Straight, and the Eyes Blue"; in *Colorado Review*, "What Was William Painting?," "When the Gods Put on Meter," "A Three-Raven Field Talking Dirty Apple Blossoms" (under the title "Stroking the Flowing Geometries"), "Rust with Night and Language in the Waste," "The Outside Butterflies Are Trying to Join the Inside Butterflies" (under the title "Throwing Like a Girl"), and "Romanza"; in *Volt*, "They Liked It Because the Wind Blew, and Blew the Birds About" (section *b*), "Feather's Wives Are All Good-Looking," and "Here's a Development"; in *Antioch Review*, "Modern Love"; in *Conduit*, "Take Me to the Godfish"; in *Interim*, "You Should See the Letters I Would Have Written If They Hadn't Agreed to Everything," "Pasting Nothing in the Wound," "Person Throwing a Stone at a Bird"; in *Barrow Street*, "Insatiability"; in *Denver Quarterly*, "Every Color Is a Wolf" (under the title "Down the Driveway of Flame and Light") and "Not Shallow Smaller but a Larger Flickering"; in *Metre* (Ireland), "Clouds of Willing Seen in the Bird Day"; in *Boston Review*, "No. 2 Pencil Quaquaversal Shout"; in *jubilat*, "They Liked It Because the Wind Blew, and Blew the Birds About" (section *a*); in *Pequod*, "Taller by the Non-Thinglike" and "Venus Rolling Up Her Stockings because of Much Memory"; in *Ploughshares*, "Icarus in Daedalus's Studio," "Open Violin Case," "Crushed Cargo," and "Jove's Thunder But a Murmur in the Leaves."

"When the Gods Put on Meter" was selected for *The Best American Poetry 2001*. "Modern Love" was reprinted in the Anniversary Issue of *The Antioch Review* (spring 2001).

My gratitude to all the editors.

The Contemporary Poetry Series • Edited by Paul Zimmer

Dannie Abse, *One-Legged on Ice*
Susan Astor, *Dame*
Gerald Barrax, *An Audience of One*
Tony Connor, *New and Selected Poems*
Franz Douskey, *Rowing Across the Dark*
Lynn Emanuel, *Hotel Fiesta*
John Engels, *Vivaldi in Early Fall*
John Engels, *Weather-Fear: New and Selected Poems, 1958–1982*
Brendan Galvin, *Atlantic Flyway*
Brendan Galvin, *Winter Oysters*
Michael Heffernan, *The Cry of Oliver Hardy*
Michael Heffernan, *To the Wreakers of Havoc*
Conrad Hilberry, *The Moon Seen as a Slice of Pineapple*
X. J. Kennedy, *Cross Ties*
Caroline Knox, *The House Party*
Gary Margolis, *The Day We Still Stand Here*
Michael Pettit, *American Light*
Bin Ramke, *White Monkeys*
J. W. Rivers, *Proud and on My Feet*
Laurie Sheck, *Amaranth*
Myra Sklarew, *The Science of Goodbyes*
Marcia Southwick, *The Night Won't Save Anyone*
Mary Swander, *Succession*
Bruce Weigl, *The Monkey Wars*
Paul Zarzyski, *The Make-Up of Ice*

The Contemporary Poetry Series • Edited by Bin Ramke

Mary Jo Bang, *The Downstream Extremity of the Isle of Swans*
J. T. Barbarese, *New Science*
J. T. Barbarese, *Under the Blue Moon*
Cal Bedient, *The Violence of the Morning*
Stephanie Brown, *Allegory of the Supermarket*
Scott Cairns, *Figures for the Ghost*
Scott Cairns, *The Translation of Babel*
Richard Chess, *Tekiah*
Richard Cole, *The Glass Children*
Martha Collins, *A History of a Small Life on a Windy Planet*
Martin Corless-Smith, *Of Piscator*
Christopher Davis, *The Patriot*
Juan Delgado, *Green Web*
Wayne Dodd, *Echoes of the Unspoken*
Wayne Dodd, *Sometimes Music Rises*
Joseph Duemer, *Customs*

Candice Favilla, *Cups*
Casey Finch, *Harming Others*
Norman Finkelstein, *Restless Messengers*
Dennis Finnell, *Belovèd Beast*
Dennis Finnell, *The Gauguin Answer Sheet*
Karen Fish, *The Cedar Canoe*
Albert Goldbarth, *Heaven and Earth: A Cosmology*
Pamela Gross, *Birds of the Night Sky/Stars of the Field*
Kathleen Halme, *Every Substance Clothed*
Jonathan Holden, *American Gothic*
Paul Hoover, *Viridian*
Austin Hummell, *The Fugitive Kind*
Claudia Keelan, *The Secularist*
Joanna Klink, *They Are Sleeping*
Maurice Kilwein Guevara, *Postmortem*
Caroline Knox, *To Newfoundland*
Steve Kronen, *Empirical Evidence*
Patrick Lawler, *A Drowning Man Is Never Tall Enough*
Sydney Lea, *No Sign*
Jeanne Lebow, *The Outlaw James Copeland and the Champion-Belted Empress*
Phillis Levin, *Temples and Fields*
Gary Margolis, *Falling Awake*
Joshua McKinney, *Saunter*
Mark McMorris, *The Black Reeds*
Jacqueline Osherow, *Conversations with Survivors*
Jacqueline Osherow, *Looking for Angels in New York*
Tracy Philpot, *Incorrect Distances*
Paisley Rekdal, *A Crash of Rhinos*
Donald Revell, *The Gaza of Winter*
Martha Ronk, *Desire in L.A.*
Martha Ronk, *Eyetrouble*
Peter Sacks, *O Wheel*
Aleda Shirley, *Chinese Architecture*
Pamela Stewart, *The Red Window*
Susan Stewart, *The Hive*
Terese Svoboda, *All Aberration*
Terese Svoboda, *Mere Mortals*
Lee Upton, *Approximate Darling*
Lee Upton, *Civilian Histories*
Arthur Vogelsang, *Twentieth Century Women*
Sidney Wade, *Empty Sleeves*
Liz Waldner, *Dark Would (the missing person)*
Marjorie Welish, *Casting Sequences*
Susan Wheeler, *Bag 'o' Diamonds*
C. D. Wright, *String Light*
Katayoon Zandvakili, *Deer Table Legs*
Andrew Zawacki, *By Reason of Breakings*